Getting Your Book Into Libraries

by

Eric Otis Simmons

ESETOMES

ESETOMES is the brand name for books written by Eric Otis Simmons. It stands for **E**ric **S**immons **E**nterprises, Inc., followed by the word **TOMES**, which is defined as one of the books in a work of several volumes.

Information provided in, "Getting Your Book Into Libraries" is intended to serve as a resource for self publishers and others seeking to market their book(s) to Libraries and presumes the purchaser has written a quality piece of work that meets the general requirements found in most Libraries' Collection Development Policy statement. Moreover, there is no guaranty the purchaser will achieve the same level of success in marketing their book(s) to Libraries as the Author. In addition to the lack of any guaranty, express or implied, there is also no express or implied Warranty. Purchaser or any third party that receives this publication from a purchaser hereby acknowledges and agrees that the Author makes no representation or warranty, express or implied, at law or in equity, in any respect to any matter relating to the contents of this publication including, without limitation, any strategy, course of action, or other undertaking.

The Purchaser hereby waives any and all claims that may arise as a result of any actions or other activities or lack of same by the Purchaser on any third party that may or may not have resulted from the content contained within this Publication. Purchaser agrees to indemnify and defend the Author, the Author's representatives, heirs, assigns, or designees against any and all claims by the Purchaser of any third party.

Dedication

This book is dedicated to my wife, Cynthia. Through our 40 years together, you have stood by my side and continued to support and encourage me in all of my endeavors, including this one.

Acknowledgments

My many thanks to noted Author Joanna Penn from TheCreativePenn.com, for sharing my article, "How To Get Your Book Into Libraries," from which this book is based, with her worldwide followers. Since the piece was released, I have received an outpouring of thanks from people around the globe for me sharing my methodology.

A special thanks also to Wanjiru Warama, whom I've never met, who read the article and messaged me on Goodreads with, "After reading the article, I thought you could have packaged it and published it as an e-book." I'm pleased to share with Ms. Warama; I have followed up on her suggestion.

About the Author

Eric Otis Simmons is an Author and owner of ESE, Inc., a website development firm specializing in creating sites for High School Athletes, seeking to get recruited by College Coaches, and Authors, Poets, and others who want to present their "Personal Brand," and value proposition, on the Internet. A former college athlete, Eric enjoys sports and public speaking.

To date, Simmons has written and self-published three other books. His Memoir, "Not Far From The Tree," the first book he had ever written, has become a multi-time Amazon "Best Seller" in the Single Parent category. "#HTSP – How to Self-Publish" takes the reader through the methodology Eric developed to write, market, and distribute his Memoir. "ESETOMES Box Set" is an eBook bundle comprised of both books.

As of this writing, **100 copies of Simmons' books have been acquired by eighty-five (85) Libraries (Academic, Public, and two Library Services companies categorized as Libraries) in**

less than two years. Of the Public Libraries that have added his books to their Collections, seven are amongst the twenty-five largest in the U.S., by volume, and includes the biggest, the New York Public Library, which purchased his Memoir and #HTSP, as he calls it, for its research arm, the prestigious Schomburg Center for Research in Black Culture. Twelve (12) Public Libraries to date have added #HTSP to their Collections, and six libraries have ordered both books. **He closed these sales without having paid for an expensive book review!**

Listed among Simmons' library customers are Howard County Library System (HCLS), Library Journal's **2013 Library of The Year** (three copies of his Memoir), Stark County District Library, a Library Journal 2018 **"Star Library"** (two copies of his Memoir), and Washington University in St. Louis, another Memoir procurer, which was listed at Number 19 in U.S. News and World Report's 2020 Best Colleges National Universities rankings. To view the list of libraries that have purchased Simmons' works, at the time of this writing, visit https://www.esetomes.com/library-customers.

Contents

Chapter 1

Why This Book?

When this book was published, if one were to Google, "Getting Your Book Into Libraries," they would get 1,050,000,000 hits, all of which would be articles and blogs on the topic. They would not find a single book in the over 1 billion hits on the subject, at least I couldn't find one, let alone a resource that was written by an author who **had gotten his books into 85 Libraries, 95% of which were closed via email contact only, within two years and did so without paying for an expensive book review!** Such a source wasn't available until now.

Admittedly, I didn't realize how much interest there was among Authors about getting their books into libraries until I wrote an article entitled, "How To Get Your Book Into Libraries," (https://www.thecreativepenn.com/2019/06/12/book-marketing-how-to-get-your-book-into-libraries/) for noted Author Joanna Penn from TheCreativePenn.com, to share with her followers around the world. When I reviewed the numbers associated with activity related to the article, I was blown away. To top it off, at one point, it seemed as though the piece had, in my view, nearly gone viral on Twitter.

I was able to determine the article's impact by doing a "before" and "after" comparison of the activity on my Author's Twitter page and Author's website starting with the day the article was posted (June 12, 2019) by Ms. Penn on her, "The Creative Penn" website through the following five months. I used a spreadsheet to track readers' reactions to the piece and kept a running total of the number of tweets, retweets, likes, mentions, shares, comments, linking site visits, new user visits, profile visits, and user sessions which I referred to as "interactions." The data was gleaned from Twitter Analytics, Google Analytics, and Google Search Console. The article continues to be well-received, and at the time of this publication has **generated 4,061 interactions from readers in thirty (30) countries!**

As the article's popularity grew, something began to gnaw at me daily. Because most "Guest" posts have a word limit, I felt my 2,000 or so words in the article had only scratched the surface as relates to the marketing tactics I had developed and the strategy I was deploying to get my books into libraries. I wanted to give Ms. Penn's readers more, and it never dawned on me to write a more in-depth version of the article in the form of a book, despite all of the justifying "interactions" data sitting right in front of me. As fate would have it, though, one day, I received a Goodreads message from a Wanjiru Warama. Ms. Warama had read, "How To Get Your Book Into Libraries," and was surprised I hadn't turned the article into a book. I got tickled because she seemed to be scolding me somewhat for not realizing I had a viable solution to address an apparent need. Ms. Warama's message was a wake-up call, and it helped me understand what had been gnawing at me. It was, I needed to write a book to further help others in getting their books into libraries.

The reason why I'm having so much success with libraries, I believe, is that I have developed a methodology that I repeat over and over again, and continue to refine. In "Getting Your Book Into

Libraries," I'm going to share with you precisely what
I'm doing.

Chapter 2

Why Try to Get Your Book Into Libraries?

Rationale

In December 2017, as I was thinking about my 2018 business goals for my Memoir, I knew I wanted to establish near irrefutable credibility around the book with potential purchasers. Ultimately, I decided to focus on libraries as a strategic "market segment" due in large part to the trustworthiness people tend to associate with these facilities, and because they have what's called a **"Collection Development Policy."** Per its website, the New Orleans Public Library, which is one of my customers, "The Collection Development Policy is designed to support the Library's Mission statement and serves as a guide for the selection, acquisition, maintenance, and retention of materials."

Having a book in a library, in my view, can help establish an Author's credibility with prospective readers because the book has been vetted by and passed a "litmus" test, so to speak, with Librarians for the work to be considered for purchase and placement within their facility. Also, libraries are highly "referenceable" customers for an Author, especially with other libraries. It has been my experience when you get your book into one library; the odds go up dramatically that others are likely to follow. I call this the "Domino Effect," and I believe it's happening with my customers. To illustrate, after initiating my "Library Campaign" in January 2018, Washington University in St. Louis became the first library to purchase my Memoir. With this "highly referenceable" account, I have been able to get twenty-two other Academic libraries to place orders for "Not Far From The Tree." When I began focusing on Public Libraries, the Detroit Public Library, the Nation's 12th largest, became my first customer in the segment. They ordered two copies of my Memoir for two Branches. Fast forward to today and fifty-nine additional Public Libraries have ordered my books. Also, after one Library Services company placed an order, so did another. There has also been one (1) independent college campus bookstore that ordered several books, but I don't count them in my Academic library totals.

Each time a Library purchases one of my books, I add them to my "Reference List" (https://www.esetomes.com/library-customers), and I share the list with prospective libraries in my introductory letters and marketing campaigns. When I was "fine-tuning" my correspondence to Librarians, I ran several campaigns where I only provided the link to my "Reference List," but my Google Analytics data showed not many Librarians were clicking on the URL, so I have gone back to inserting the "List" in my emails.

One clear benefit I have seen from providing library references is a shorter time to sales closure, particularly with Public Libraries, which is now down from a six-month purchase cycle to three months on average. Also and remarkably, **17 libraries purchased after one contact!**

The Library Market

Per a spreadsheet on the Internet developed by the Online Computer Library Center (OCLC) entitled, "Country Data for OCLC Web," in 2016, there were

1.4 million libraries worldwide, and of these 336,841 were Academic and Public (45,028 and 291,813 respectively) facilities. In the U.S., the data showed 3,793 Academic and 9,042 Public libraries, which closely mirrors the American Library Association's (ALA) numbers. Note: I consider the Public Library "Market Opportunity" in the U.S. as 16,568, which is the total number of buildings per ALA. In November 2019, the International Federation of Library Associations and Institution's (IFLA) "Library Map of The World" revealed the number of Libraries worldwide had grown to 2.6 million, and of these, there were 80,078 Academic and 405,048 Public Libraries around the globe (485,126 total). I don't focus on School Libraries (Public, Private, and Bureau of Indian Affairs, here in the U.S.), but IFLA's Map shows there are 2 million such libraries around the world. ALA shows there are 98,460 School Libraries in the U.S., which is eight (8) times the number of Public and Academic Libraries in the country combined. So, as you can see, the library market is enormous!

LIBRARY MAP OF THE WORLD

IFLA Library Map of the World is a representative source of basic library statistics and a robust tool providing country-level data and a worldwide comparison of different library performance metrics by region.

Metric **Number of Libraries**
Country **All Countries**
Numbering System **Totals by Country**
Library Type **National Libraries, Academic Libraries, Public Libraries, Community Libraries, School Libraries, Other Libraries**

Number of Libraries
A library is an organization, or part of an organization, the main aim of which is to facilitate the use of such information resources, services and facilities as are required to meet the informational, research, educational, cultural or recreational needs of its users (to read the full description please go to the Glossary page in the About section of the site).

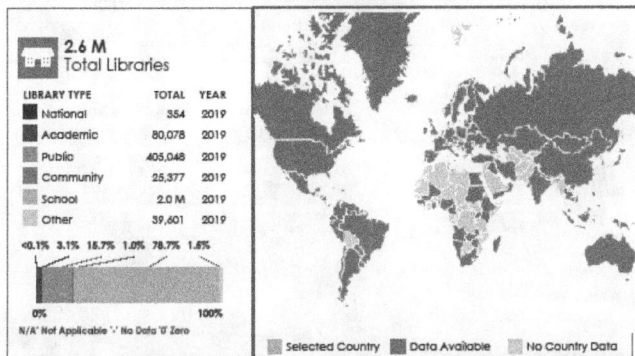

2.6 M Total Libraries

LIBRARY TYPE	TOTAL	YEAR
National	354	2019
Academic	80,078	2019
Public	405,048	2019
Community	25,377	2019
School	2.0 M	2019
Other	39,601	2019

<0.1% 3.1% 18.7% 1.0% 78.7% 1.6%

0%   100%
N/A 'Not Applicable '-' No Data '0' Zero

Selected Country   Data Available   No Country Data

	Number of Libraries	Libraries w/ Internet	Full-Time Staff	Volunteers	Registered Users	Physical Visits	Physical Loans	Electronic Loans
Worldwide Totals	2.6 M	377,840	1.6 M	845,469	1,114.8 M	6,296.8 M	9,363.1 M	13,081.7 M
Africa	109,241	27,864	20,037	579	6.9 M	190.3 M	111.0 M	10.6 M
Asia	1.9 M	82,760	636,426	634,137	546.8 M	1,526.9 M	3,039.5 M	10,653.2 M
Europe	296,844	143,427	496,611	206,099	195.1 M	2,318.3 M	3,278.4 M	1,495.0 M
Oceania	14,380	4,372	25,481	36	17.2 M	210.7 M	211.8 M	2.2 M
Northern America	129,129	97,988	303,490	1,475	191.9 M	1,729.3 M	2,576.5 M	226.1 M
Latin America & Caribbean	146,429	21,429	91,239	3,143	156.8 M	311.1 M	135.9 M	692.5 M

(Downloadable image courtesy of IFLA)

If you are targeting millennials for your books, they are more likely than older generations to say libraries help them find trustworthy information, learn new things, and make informed decisions, per a 2016 Pew Research Center survey.

Millennials more likely than older generations to say libraries help them find trustworthy information, learn new things and make informed decisions

% of adults who say they think the public library helps them ...

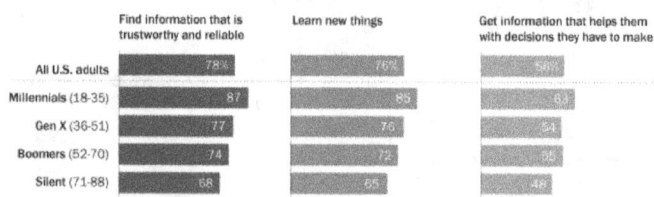

	Find information that is trustworthy and reliable	Learn new things	Get information that helps them with decisions they have to make
All U.S. adults	78%	76%	56%
Millennials (18-35)	87	85	63
Gen X (36-51)	77	76	54
Boomers (52-70)	74	72	55
Silent (71-88)	68	65	48

Source: Survey conducted Sept. 29-Nov. 6, 2016.
PEW RESEARCH CENTER

(Downloadable image courtesy of Pew Research Center)

On February 22, 2017, Reedsy published an article (https://blog.reedsy.com/libraries-self-publishing-authors/), which stated, " ... 92% of librarians surveyed between May 2016 – July 2016 by New Shelves noted that they regularly buy books from self-published authors and small presses. The article goes on to say, "Once one library has your book and the check-out rates start showing up on reports, other librarians will start ordering your book. The growth and spread of your book's sales and popularity will start happening while you are not even looking!"

The Challenge

You will find some Librarians still rely heavily on book reviews. As evidence, one Librarian sent me the following in an email last year, "New library materials are considered for purchase using a variety of selection criteria including favorable reviews in standard library review media (Library Journal, Kirkus, Booklist) anticipated demand for the material, local interest, and space and budgetary considerations."

Personally, I struggle mightily with book reviews. Here's why. Per Kirkus' website, as of this writing, the charge for a "Traditional Review" is $425 U.S., and you can expect a 250-300 word review back in 7-9 weeks. If you want your review expedited, the cost is $575. A second option is an "Expanded Review" that can be received in 7-9 weeks for $575, and for an expedited review, the cost is $725. At a royalty rate of let's say, $3.00 U.S. for a paperback book, one would have to sell roughly 142 books to break even on the

"Traditional Review." That's like giving 142 Libraries a book for free! At this juncture, I prefer not to "pay to play," if you will, to get my works into libraries because the fees are more than I'm currently willing to pay. Thanks, but no thanks!! I do realize, however, my stubbornness could be costing me revenue. Let's assume a Kirkus "Traditional Review" yielded me, 1,000 new library customers. Using the previous $3.00 royalty rate, I might be missing out on a net revenue gain of $2,575 ($3,000-$425).

In my article for Ms. Penn, I stated, "Due to my current "marketing" budget, however, I'm staying pat for now on paying for a book review." After the article was posted, Publishers Weekly (PW) announced on its BookLife website, Fiction and Nonfiction Contests called The BookLife Prize, in which the grand prize was $5,000. BookLife is a Publishers Weekly site dedicated to Indie Authors (i.e., self-publishers) where they can submit their self-published books to PW for review consideration, or they can purchase a BookLife Review for, "$399 for a complete review ... written by an expert Publishers Weekly reviewer, with a six-week turnaround time." The BookLife Prize had an entry fee of $99 per book, and all entrants were to receive a Critic's Report, which was described as a brief critical assessment of their manuscript written by a Publishers Weekly reviewer. The $99 cost for a review was the lowest price I had seen in the past two years from an entity that Librarians are familiar with and one in which they might use when assessing a book(s) for purchase.

Admittedly, I viewed the "brief critical assessment" statement as a red flag and felt a submitted manuscript might only be briefly scanned and not completely read by a reviewer. Ultimately, I did pony up the $99 though and entered "Not Far From The Tree" into the contest. To be on the safe side, in case my entry was merely skimmed through and not fully read, I placed in the front of my submission, a ten-page chapter by chapter summary. Surely a reviewer would read ten pages, was my line of thinking. After I receive the "brief critical assessment," which I believe will be positive, my strategy is to use the "review" as a marketing tool with Librarians. Going back to my $3.00 royalty rate example, let's say the "brief critical assessment" resulted in one book sold per library, then it would take 33 libraries for me to break even on my

$99 BookLife contest entry fee. I believe closing 33 new libraries, via the review, is achievable because I'm currently closing 42 libraries a year without a review.

Book Review Resources

Should you opt for a book review before you start engaging libraries, the following list of resources from IngramSpark should be of assistance. IngramSpark, a self-publishing platform provider, points out you should keep in mind many of these publications require submission before a book's publication.

Booklist: Adult and Youth | Circulation: 80,000 print; 160,000 online

Library Journal: Adult | Circulation: 100,000

Library Journal Self-e program: Adult and Youth self-published eBooks

Publishers Weekly and PW Children's: Adult and Youth | Circulation: 25,000

School Library Journal: Youth titles | Circulation: 33,000 print; 44,000 online

Voice of Youth Advocates (VOYA): Young Adult |
Circulation: 7,000

Choice Magazine: Academic | Circulation: 22,000
librarians and faculty

The Bulletin of the Center for Children's Books: Youth
| Circulation: 2,000

Horn Book: Youth | Circulation: 13,000

Kirkus Reviews: Adult and Youth | Circulation: 3,000
print

I would also suggest you keep an eye out for contests
like BookLife's because you might be able to find a
"review" at a discounted price.

Chapter 3

Getting Started Marketing to Libraries

To get your book(s) into libraries, you're going to have to develop a strategy for contacting Librarians. Before getting started, you'll need to get answers to two key questions. 1). Who are the primary decision-makers in the libraries you'll be contacting, and 2). Where do these libraries go to purchase their books?

Key Decision Makers in a Library

Depending on the size of a Library, the key decision-makers will have titles such as Head Librarian, Director, Branch Manager, or in the case of Academic libraries, perhaps Dean. Other vital titles are Collection Development Librarian or Acquisitions Librarian. If it's a large library, don't be surprised if the Collection Development Librarian has the latitude to make the final decision on a book purchase. This individual carries a lot of weight, and quite often, the Head Librarian will refer you to the Collections Development Librarian. You should also look for

16

potential "influencers" in a Library. If a Librarian has responsibility for children's books, and you've written one, that person needs to be on your contact list. So, genre responsibility is essential, as well. Do sell "top-down," i.e., to the highest titled person in the Library. The rationale here is the "boss" can override a subordinate's decision - if you catch my drift. For large libraries, I try to have at least two contacts, and for some, I have more because my thinking is, individual Librarians may decide to make a personal purchase, as was the case with a Global Education Librarian at a University. Her school also bought a book, so because I thought "out of the box," in terms of reaching out to others outside of the standard "decision tree," I was able to get two sales.

How Do Libraries Select Books?

While Libraries' Collection Development Policies may differ based on a variety of factors such as Patron demographics, etc., the American Library Association (ALA) has "suggested guidelines" if you will, for Public, School, and Academic Libraries in a document

entitled,   "Selection   Criteria"
(http://www.ala.org/tools/challengesupport/selectio
npolicytoolkit/criteria).   While not all-inclusive, I've
listed some of the criteria that stand out to me as a self-
publisher.

General Criteria

- Suitability of subject and style for intended audience
- Exhibit a high degree of potential user appeal and interest
- Scope and content
- Meet high standards in literary, artistic, and aesthetic quality; technical aspects; and physical format

Content Criteria

- Skill, competence, and purpose of the author
- Vitality and originality
- Clarity
- Sustained interest

I believe if an Author understands where their book(s) fit within a library's Collection Development Policy, they can use that knowledge to show Librarians how their book(s) align with the Policy. To illustrate, I reside in Metro Atlanta, and I wanted to get my books into every library in Fulton County Library System, which has thirty-four Branches. Cognizant Atlanta proper has a sizeable minority population; I sought to educate myself on the System's Collection Development Policy as relates to diversity. Upon reading the material, one section stated, "The library will, therefore, seek to acquire, organize, disseminate, and preserve information resources that are both relevant to the advancement of human knowledge in general and specific to the particular needs of our diverse, metropolitan community." Following, I did some demographic research to build a case showing why my Memoir would be a good fit for the System's "diverse" community. As a part of my "value proposition," I created a map (see the following image) of every city where my book had been purchased by a library or System whose demographics were similar to Atlanta's. My subsequent email Subject line read, "Demographics of Libraries Purchasing "Not Far From The Tree" Mirror Atlanta." I began my correspondence with, "To ensure "Not Far From The Tree" would be a good fit for the communities Fulton County Library System serves, I reviewed the African American demographics of libraries that have purchased my Memoir and compared the data to the city of Atlanta's African American demographics. The numbers are virtually identical with the African American population of my current Public Library customers averaging 37% as compared to 38% for Atlanta."

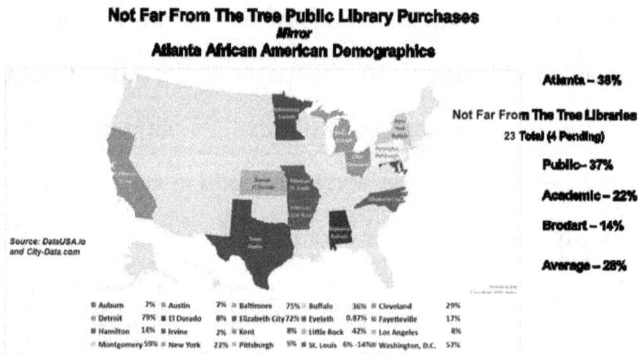

Not Far From The Tree Public Library Purchases
Mirror
Atlanta African American Demographics

After two years of trying to get my Memoir into Fulton County, the System purchased the eBook

version of the book shortly after receipt of my
"justification" letter. I'm convinced showing how my
manuscript aligned with the library's Collection
Development Policy is what helped closed the deal.
Now that I have my "foot in the door," I plan to
engage all of the System's Branches because now I
have the System itself as a reference.

I don't go into as much in-depth research for every
library as I did for Fulton County, but if a System has
ten or more Branches, I may.

Where Do Libraries Go to Purchase Their Books?

Libraries purchase their books from a variety of
sources. Two of the most common companies you'll
hear about are Baker & Taylor and Ingram Content
Group, also known as Ingram. According to its
website, Baker & Taylor is a premier provider of
books, digital content, and technology solutions that
help Public Libraries improve community outcomes
through literacy and learning. Per Wikipedia, Ingram
has the industry's most extensive active book inventory

with access to 7.5 million titles, and the markets they serve include booksellers, Librarians, educators, and specialty retailers. IngramSpark, a division of Ingram, differs from free self-publishing platforms in that it has a setup fee of $49 per print book, currently, or $49 for print and eBook when uploaded at the same time, or $25 for an eBook. I am presently only using their print book option for my books at this time. Some other sources libraries procure from and that I'm using, include Amazon, via its Kindle Direct Publishing's (KDP) Expanded Distribution offering, Smashwords, Draft2Digital, and StreetLib. Also, Blurb appears to be the source of my latest Library Services purchase, but I will have to confirm. Each of these companies offers free self-publishing platforms, as well.

Baker & Taylor (B&T) seems to be the preferred vendor of many Librarians, but in my case, most of my library customers have purchased the paperback versions of my books from Ingram. I anticipate my B&T sales will begin to pick up dramatically now that an error has been corrected. To make a long story short, my books got dropped by B&T when CreateSpace, KDP's predecessor, was absorbed by

KDP. To complicate matters, KDP was not doing business with B&T at the time, and may still not be. In any event, I ended up reaching out to B&T directly, and after about four months, I was able to get my books added back into their system. Note, although Ingram distributes through B&T, the company states on its website, "Since B&T targets libraries, they may decide to not to carry a specific title-- regardless of the printer or publisher--if they feel it won't generate interest from their target audience. We cannot *make* B&T carry a title. It is completely at the discretion of B&T." So my take is, if B&T doesn't pick up your self-published title through Ingram, you may have to reach out to B&T directly or try to get a library to request your book from them.

In terms of my paperback library sales through KDP's Expanded Distribution offering, they have been minimal, as has been the case with Brodart, another procurement company some Librarians use for book purchases. As for my eBooks, I've had sales to the Los Angeles Public Library (the U.S.' 5th largest Public Library) and others through OverDrive, a service that allows customers to borrow digital content from a library for free. My Overdrive sales have come through Draft2Digital (D2D), Smashwords, and StreetLib. Last year, D2D began working with Bibliotheca, a Library management solutions company, which unlike Overdrive, you can get a royalty payment when your eBook is checked out. D2D calls this option Cost Per Checkout (CPC), which they describe as "CPC allows libraries to have access to the same title for more than one user. Instead of a fixed price, libraries gain access to your books and pay 1/10 of the book's full purchase price, each time it is loaned out." To date, I've received several small royalty payments under this option and wish OverDrive and Bibliotheca offered a royalty for a book's purchase plus a CPC royalty for each checkout.

Chapter 4

Building Your "Library Contacts Database"

Aside from you and your books, your "Library Contacts Database" will be your most valuable asset in helping to facilitate your success in marketing to libraries. I consider my "Database" as "golden," and without it, I would not have been able to close as many library sales as I have.

I built my "Library Contacts Database" with Microsoft Excel. This "spreadsheet on steroids," as I call it, contains all of my library contacts, and I've set it up to be sortable by field. When I wrote "How To Get Your Book Into Libraries," the "Database" contained 2,187 libraries and had 2,046 Academic Library contacts and 1,069 Public Library contacts, which equated to 1.4 contacts per library. I've grown the total number of contacts in the "Database" to 4,371, as of this writing.

In the spreadsheet, I keep separate tabs for my Academic and Public libraries because this makes it easier for me to do "targeted" mass mailings to either sector.   Construct-wise, the spreadsheet has the following field headings: Status (so I can input whether I've checked to see if a library has purchased one of my books), State, Library Type (i.e., Public or Academic), Library Link (i.e., URL), First Name, Last Name, Salutation (example Mary, or Dr. Smith), Email Address, Date Contacted, Library Name, and Notes. In the Notes field, I put the name of the consortium, if the library belongs to one, so that I can email all of the group's members during a "targeted" marketing campaign. The same applies to Library Systems, with a large number of Branches.

When I initially began my "Library Campaign," my goal was to get my Memoir in front of the biggest libraries in America. I started by Googling, "largest libraries in the United States."   One of the search results yielded, "List of the largest libraries in the United States – Wikipedia." On the page, there were several lists that I copied and pasted into a spreadsheet that would later become my "Library Contacts Database." Next, I went onto each library's website and searched for their decision-makers. This one by one method of finding contact information proved to be a long and arduous process, though. I knew there had to be a better way. Over time, I discovered some states list their libraries and library directors on the state's government site. The contacts might be available via a downloadable spreadsheet or PDF document. On a few occasions, I found Excel worksheets that were several years old, just sitting out on the Internet.

To give you an example of a state that lists Librarians' contact information, I'll use Alabama, which is where I lived for about twenty years and was the first state that I targeted for my library marketing efforts. My Google search results from my entry of, "list of library directors in Alabama," yielded over twenty million hits. I honed in on the top three results, which were:

- Directory of Public Libraries in Alabama
- Alabama Public Libraries
- Alabama Public Library Service

The Alabama Public Library Service had precisely the information I was seeking. On the site's landing page, next to the "Home" tab, there was a tab that read, "Public Library Listings." The listing had every Public Library in the state along with the Library's website address, if there was one, phone number, Director's name, and email address (see the following image). All I had to do was copy and paste each row into my "Database."

The State of North Carolina also had easily accessible information. When I searched for "state of North Carolina libraries and librarian contacts," one of the Google hits was, "Library Directory | State Library of North Carolina." Every Academic and Public Library in the State of North Carolina and its Head Librarian was listed, plus there was a downloadable spreadsheet to boot! Now, before you get overly excited, Alabama and North Carolina are more of an exception than the rule. For many of the libraries and their contacts in my "Database," I had to do a lot of manual copying and pasteing, at a rate of adding about twelve (12) libraries an hour, I might add. As a result, when I am looking to add a new state to my spreadsheet, I prioritize adding those states that have spreadsheet-like formats first.

When I began focusing on Public Library's, I came across a site, "LibWeb, Library Servers via WWW" (https://www.lib-web.org/united-states/public-libraries) on which you can click on a particular U.S. State, and be directed to Public Libraries within the State. Next, you click on a Library's link, and you will be taken to the Library's home page. Now, you will have to search the site to identify the primary decision-maker(s). In many cases, the decision-makers can be found under "About Us," "Staff Directory," or similar. LibWeb also lists Academic libraries in the same manner   (https://www.lib-web.org/united-states/academic-libraries.)   While adding contacts under this scenario is more time consuming than is the case when a state has a spreadsheet with contacts available, I wanted to make you aware of this site because the list of libraries is robust. To give you a feel for what my "Library Contacts Database" looks like, I've provided the following screenshot.

Chapter 5

Creating a "Mail Merge" Document

After Librarians' contact information has been loaded into my "Database" to correspond with them, individually or in mass, via email, I do so via Microsoft Word's "Step-by-Step Mail Merge Wizard." If you are unfamiliar with how to do a Word "Mail Merge," Google, "Mail merge using an Excel spreadsheet - Word - Office Support," and Microsoft has instructions that will show you how. There will also be some YouTube videos that the search will reveal.

Through "Mail Merge," I can customize my "Campaign" letters so that they look "tailored" for the specific individual versus having a "mass email" look. I can insert the Librarian's first name or title and the Library's name in the body of the document if I like. Before embarking on an email campaign to Librarians, be sure to look into the daily email limits of your provider. I learned the hard way that my Microsoft Outlook email account has a daily limit, under my Office 365 subscription, of 300 emails per day. I tried to do a mailing of over 300 once, and I got locked out of my account.

Earlier, I mentioned my "Library Contacts Database" is sortable. To give you an example of how I use the sorting capability, let's say I want to email Ohio libraries to make them aware there are currently sixteen libraries in the state that have purchased my books. First, I add a new tab to the "Database" that I name, Ohio Mailing, for instance. Next, I copy and paste the field headings I mentioned in Chapter 4, into the first row of the worksheet in the new tab. I go back to my contacts list and sort by state and then cut and paste all of the Ohio contacts into the new Ohio Mailing tab. Next, I create my email in Microsoft Word. In the body of the email, I will copy and paste the libraries in Ohio that have purchased one or more of my books, from my "Libraries With ESETOMES Books," spreadsheet, which is where I keep all of the libraries that have made a purchase. Lastly, I use Word's "Mail Merge" function to send out my emails.

I try to be creative with my "messaging" in the Subject line of my emails. For this example, I might put in the Subject line something like, "16 Ohio

Libraries Add Books by Eric Otis Simmons." Or, I might put, "Not Far From The Tree" Popular With 16 Ohio Libraries." My "hooks" to get the recipient to open the email are my mentioning of the state of Ohio and the quantification of the number of libraries in Ohio that have purchased my books (i.e.,16).

Using the example above, in addition to sharing my Ohio references with the Librarians, I want to promote "#HTSP - How to Self-Publish." The body of the email would be mostly the same, including the list of 16 Ohio customers, but in my heading, my "hook" could be the inclusion of an Ohio library that has purchased the book such as MidPointe Library System. In the Subject line of the email, I could put something like MidPointe Library System Adds "#HTSP – How to Self-Publish." Or I could put in the Subject line, "Patrons at MidPointe Like #HTSP – How to Self-Publish," which has two "hooks." One is the use of the word "Patrons" (i.e., the visitors to a library), and the other is the name of a referenceable Ohio library. Note, I wouldn't have to use MidPointe's full name in the subject line because the recipient will know by the spelling it's a peer Ohio library. Also, I would have previously checked MidPointe's website, and known #HTSP had been checked out on several occasions by the Library's Patrons.

Chapter 6

Tactics

To help you better understand the tactics I'm using to get my books into libraries, I put together a graphical depiction, which I believe captures the essence of what I'm doing. I also wanted the description to be "catchy" so that it might be easy for you to retain. In a nutshell, my methodology is Research, Initiate, Review and Revise, Reinitiate, Repeat. I'll explain each.

- **Research** – do some homework before engaging the customer. For instance, you might learn from a library's website that they belong to a consortium. You may decide to contact the consortium and all of its members with the thinking, if one member purchases, others are likely to follow

- **Initiate** – begin contacting libraries

- **Review and Revise** – assess what happened when you made contact. Use what you reviewed to modify what you previously did so that you can improve results. A good example here is, Google Analytics revealed Librarians were not clinking on my "References" link; so, I went back to inputting the library "References" list in my correspondence

- **Reinitiate** – implement your revisions

- **Repeat** – continue doing all of the above and keep refining even after you've had some success

Eric's Library Tactics

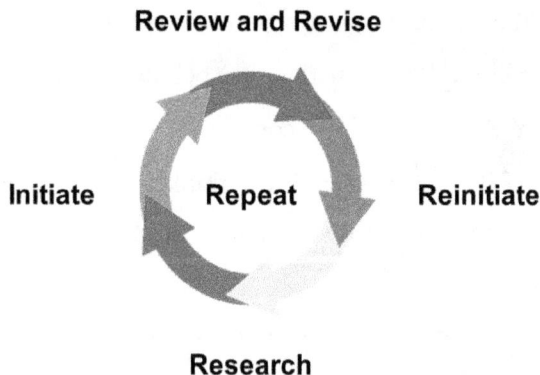

Review and Revise

Initiate   **Repeat**   **Reinitiate**

Research

Email Content

As shared, emails are my primary method for contacting libraries (i.e., Librarians). If you are wondering why I don't make a lot of phone calls, well, back in January 2018, when I first started reaching out to libraries, I did both emailing and phone calls. Invariably when I would call, I would be asked to send over my information, so I would end up having to send an email anyway. Also, there are just too many libraries out there to try and call one by one.

An Academic Librarian provided her perspective about emails in a comment to my article on Ms. Penn's website. She wrote, "If you really must e-mail a librarian directly, try approaching it like this "my book relates to this area or class that I see is offered at your institution, if you have a moment, please take a look at my reviews (link) to see if this title would be a good fit for your collection" rather than outright requesting it be added to the collection." What jumped out at me in the comment was, "... **my book relates to this area or class.**" That's the key for us, Authors, I believe! We have to be able to show Librarians the **connection** that exists between our books and their libraries' needs. When I think about it, my use of library references, in my emails, is creating a connection between my books and the Collection Development Policy around, "Exhibit a high degree of potential user appeal and interest," for example. By showing the list of libraries that have purchased my books, I'm conveying, "My books have appeal, and they are generating interest."

The underlying construct of my emails has remained virtually unchanged since 2018. I try to incorporate an attention-grabbing subject line, share "success" information about my book(s), include sales performance, add an image, such as an Amazon "Best Seller" screenshot, provide library references, share where my book(s) can be purchased, list their ISBNs, and include my Author's website beneath my signature line. Some of my emails may not include all of the elements, but I can pick and choose from the list.

If you don't have a library reference, the other items are still applicable, I feel. For sales information, I use my books' Amazon performance, which I keep track of in a spreadsheet. I get the data from "Author Central," which I check at least once a day. Whenever my paperback sales go up, for instance, and the arrow has turned green, in Author Central, I note my ranking number, which in the case of paperbacks is out of over 8,000,000 books sold worldwide on Amazon.com, per the Best Seller ranking page. So let's say my Memoir reached a ranking of 109,306 today. It's worldwide ranking put it in the "Top 1.4" of all books sold worldwide on Amazon's site, if even for an hour. I use this positive development and might say in an email, "This month, "Not Far From The Tree" peaked at being ranked in the "Top 1.4%" out of over 8,000,000 books sold worldwide on Amazon.com." Following is an example of how I show several months of sales performance in an email:

Recent *Not Far From The Tree* Amazon.com Sales Performance:

- October 9, 2019 **"Top 1.4%"** (number 109,306)
- September 19, 2019 **"Top 1.5%"** (number 118,589)
- August 3, 2019 **"Top 1.6%"** (number 126,922)
- July 14, 2019 **"Top 1.2%"** (number 95,722)
- April 19, 2019 **"Top 1.5%"** (number 121,399)
- March 3, 2019 **"Top 1.6%"** (number 130,743)

Should the Libraries I'm contacting have "book appeal" in their Collection Development Policies, which I believe most will, I'm addressing the requirement by providing factual and quantitative sales information from a known source (i.e., Amazon).

Which Libraries Should You Target First?

I suggest you target libraries in the area in which you were born, the area in which you currently reside, your local and area Public and Academic libraries, and previous locations in which you lived, first. The reason being, if you have written a quality piece of work, libraries that you have a "geographic" connection with may be more inclined to consider your book(s) and support you. In my case, I've found many libraries to be supportive of "local" Authors and those with "geographic" ties. The Public Library in Little Rock, Arkansas, where I was born, purchased my Memoir after I made them aware, I was a "native son." The Montgomery City-County Public Library, where my Mother and I moved to when I was thirteen, purchased four copies of my Memoir and one copy of #HTSP.

In addition to the local/geographic tie(s), you might get invited to speak about your book, which is what happened to me with my local Public Library.

When's the Best Time to Sell to Libraries?

Libraries tend to buy year-round, but by and large, I've found the briskest selling times to be during their Fiscal Year-End/Fiscal Year Begin (FYE/FYB). It varies, but most of the libraries I've contacted, to date, seem to have their FYE/FYB between April and July. In May 2019, the Institute of Museum and Library Services provided a listing of the Fiscal Years for Public Libraries, by state, for the year 2017. My guess is the information is still pretty accurate, and I plan to focus my future FYE/FYB marketing campaigns to Public Libraries around the dates.

Table 2. Reporting Periods of Public Libraries, by State: FY 2017

July 2016 through June 2017	January 2017 through December 2017	October 2016 through September 2017	Other[1]
Arizona	Arkansas	Alabama	Alaska[2]
California	Colorado	District of Columbia	Illinois[3]
Connecticut	Indiana	Florida	Maine[4]
Delaware	Kansas	Idaho	Michigan[5]
Georgia	Louisiana	Mississippi	Missouri[6]
Hawaii	Minnesota	American Samoa	Nebraska[7]
Iowa	New Jersey	Guam	New Hampshire[8]
Kentucky	North Dakota	Northern Marianas	New York[9]
Maryland	Ohio		Texas[10]
Massachusetts	Pennsylvania		Utah[8]
Montana	South Dakota		Vermont[7]
Nevada	Washington		
New Mexico	Wisconsin		
North Carolina			
Oklahoma			
Oregon			
Rhode Island			
South Carolina			
Tennessee			
Virginia			
West Virginia			
Wyoming			

[1] The reporting period varies among localities for the states in this column; however, each public library provided data for a 12-month period.
[2] January 2016 to June 2017.
[3] December 2015 to June 2017.
[4] April 2016 to December 2017.
[5] December 2015 to September 2017.
[6] January 2016 to October 2017.
[7] January 2016 to December 2017.
[8] July 2016 to December 2017.
[9] April 2016 to December 2017.
[10] February 2016 to December 2017.
SOURCE: IMLS, Public Libraries Survey, FY 2017.

7

Source: Institute of Museum and Library Services – "Public Libraries Survey Fiscal Year 2017" (Published May 2019)

I have found the two months leading up to FYE, the month of FYB, and the month following as good times to approach Librarians because they will be spending both remaining and new funds.

Marketing Campaigns

I try to run a library marketing campaign at least every two months, and I rotate through my "Library Contacts Database." The only time I try to contact all of the libraries in the "Database" is when I have a significant price promotion, or I've written a new book, or I have a new purchasing resource that's picked up my book that Librarians will be familiar with such as Baker & Taylor, for instance. Otherwise, I'm doing "Targeted" campaigns where I'm focusing on, for example, a specific state like North Carolina where my "Introductory" email resulted in the purchase of five copies of "#HTSP - How to Self-Publish," by a Public Library System. Some of the Subject line headings for my email marketing campaigns have been:

- Introducing "Not Far From The Tree" and "#HTSP - How to Self-Publish"

- Introducing an Amazon "Best Seller" and 2 Other Works by Eric Otis Simmons at 15% Off

- "Not Far From The Tree" Baker & Taylor Availability and "Spring Break" Promo

- Fall Kick-Off - 15% Off "Not Far From The Tree" and Other Works by Eric Otis Simmons

In "The Science Behind Email Open Rates (and How to Get More People to Read Your Emails)," Steven MacDonald wrote, "… in 2019, **the average email open rate dropped to 22.1%**." I'm not trying to be "sneaky" by using multiple email addresses, but, if an email is the best way for me to get information about my books in front of Librarians, and the most productive, I've got to find creative ways to do so because I believe my works merit their attention.

Consider Using Multiple Email Addresses

Although this tactic might not go over well with Librarians, you may want to consider using multiple email addresses to contact libraries. I use three different email addresses. Why? 1) To avoid the appearance of bombarding the email recipient, 2) If I want to send more than 300 emails at a time and 3) As a backup plan in case my email gets put in a "junk email" list. I'm not trying to be "sneaky" here, but, if an email is the best way for me to get information about my books in front of Librarians, and the most productive, I've got to find creative ways to do so because I believe my works merit their attention.

Purchase a Library Mailing List

For my "How To Get Your Book Into Libraries" article, I did some research to see if there were library mailing lists that you could purchase and located one provided by Lists You Can Afford. At the time, the site listed library contacts ranging from 900 to 23,000, with prices from $39 to $99.

If you're looking for a vetted list that is generating proven results for a self-publisher, however, my "Library Contacts Database," that I made available to Ms. Penn's followers, which contains just over 3,000 contacts, is available to you as well for $19.97. You can order from https://www.esetomes.com/product-page/library-contacts-database. My "North Carolina Library Campaign" shell letter is also included. Now that my "Database" is over 4,000 contacts, I plan to add a second offering at a price yet to be determined, so do check the above link periodically, if you are interested.

Chapter 7

Summary of My "Secret Sauce"

Now you have my "Secret Sauce," if you will, as to the tactics I've been using to get my books into libraries. To summarize, they are:

- Bring to the table a well-written piece of work and try to find a connection between it and libraries' Collection Development Policy

- Identify the primary decision-makers in a library and sell from the "Top Down"

- Utilize a "Library Contacts Database"

- Become proficient in Mail Merge so that you can send out "customized" emails

- Incorporate an image, use quantitative data, and provide references in your correspondence

- **Research, Initiate, Review and Revise, Reinitiate, Repeat**

Thank You!

My sincere thanks to you for your purchase, and here's wishing you the best of luck in selling to libraries.

Respectfully,

Eric

Other Works by Eric Otis Simmons

(www.esetomes.com)

Not Far From The Tree

How does a child raised by a single-parent African American Mother go on to graduate in the "Top 10%" of his college class, walk-on and play college basketball, become President of his IBM sales training class, close sales of $1/2 million, $1 million, and $25 million in Paris, Brussels, and Hong Kong and self-publish a "**Best Seller**" book? Fueled by his Mom's mantra, "You can do anything if you put your mind to it," and other "seeds of knowledge"

48

ingrained in him by her, Eric Otis Simmons went on to accomplish all of the above and more!

#HTSP – How to Self-Publish

A concise 79-page "how-to" book that can be used as a resource or "primer" by first-time self publishers and others interested in self publishing. Simmons shares the methodology he developed for "Not Far From The Tree," his successful Amazon "Best Seller" Memoir.

ESETOMES Box Set

An eBook "box set," or bundle, containing *Not Far From The Tree* and *#HTSP - How to Self-Publish* at 15% off retail.

References

- TheCreativePenn.com – "How To Get Your Book Into Libraries" by Eric Otis Simmons (https://www.thecreativepenn.com/2019/06/12/book-marketing-how-to-get-your-book-into-libraries/)

- New Orleans Public Library website (http://www.nolalibrary.org/)

- Online Computer Library Center (OCLC) - https://www.oclc.org/en/home.html

- Wikipedia

- IngramSpark.com – "How Indie Authors Can Get Their Books Into Libraries" by Robin Cutler

- The International Federation of Library Associations and Institutions (IFLA) – "Library Map of The World" (downloaded on November 18, 2019)

- Pew Research Center – "Most Americans – especially Millennials – say libraries can help them find reliable, trustworthy information" by A.W. Geiger

- ReedsyBlog – "5 Reasons Why Selling to Libraries Needs to be a Top Priority" by Amy Collins (February 22, 2017)

- KirkusReviews.com

- BookLife.com

- American Library Association – "Selection Criteria" http://www.ala.org/tools/challengesupport/selectionpolicytoolkit/criteria

- Baker & Taylor - https://www.baker-taylor.com/

- Institute of Museum and Library Services – "Public Libraries Survey Fiscal Year 2017" (Published May 2019)

- SuperOffice.com - "The Science Behind Email Open Rates (and How to Get More People to Read Your Emails)" by Steven MacDonald https://www.superoffice.com/blog/email-open-rates/

References

- Fulton County Library System website (http://afpls.org/)